HOW TO WIN A STREET FIGHT

UNARMED SELF DEFENSE AND STREET FIGHTING
TACTICS

SAM FURY

Illustrated by
SHUMONA MALLICK

WARNINGS AND DISCLAIMERS

The information in this publication is made public for reference only.

Neither the author, publisher, nor anyone else involved in the production of this publication is responsible for how the reader uses the information or the result of his/her actions.

CONTENTS

THANKS FOR YOUR PURCHASE

Did you know you can get FREE chapters of any SF Nonfiction Book you want?

https://offers.SFNonfictionBooks.com/Free-Chapters

You will also be among the first to know of FREE review copies, discount offers, bonus content, and more.

Go to:

https://offers.SFNonfictionBooks.com/Free-Chapters

Thanks again for your support.

INTRODUCTION

I hope you find the information inside useful.

Please remember that the techniques inside this book are not to be used likely.

When training please be careful, and if you have to use them in a real street fight (hopefully you are never in such a situation), please be mindful of use of force.

In most cases it is best to not fight.

The techniques are presented in the order you should learn them according to strategy.

SAFETY

Follow these guidelines to get the most out of training in a safe manner.

- Use proper equipment where applicable e.g. mats, training weapons, protective equipment etc.
- Wear appropriate clothing, no jewelry.
- Train for reality, but only use enough force to get the desired effect.
- Put safety before pride. 'Tap out' before you need to.
- Don't train on injuries.
- Get injuries checked out by a professional ASAP to prevent them from getting worse.
- Ensure you are physically ready before you begin training. If you have any doubts, see your physician.
- Warm up, cool down and stretch.

TRAINING METHODS

Shadow Boxing

Shadow Boxing is practicing to fight against an imaginary enemy. It needs no equipment (although a mirror can be useful). Do it slowly to learn/improve technique or increase speed for a warm up or an aerobic workout. Imagine a scenario e.g. multiple opponents, and react as you should according to the strategy.

Reaction Training

One person attacks and the other person reacts. It can be combined with pad work. The parameters of attack and response are decided upon before-hand and protective equipment should be considered.

Sparring

To spar is to fight against one or more partners for training purposes. Conditional variations are limited only to your imagination e.g. hands only, feet only, eyes closed, anything but weapons, just ground fighting, first to take-down, first to get the weapon, anything goes etc.

Start slowly. As skills improve, speed can be increased. As fitness builds, timed rounds can be increased.

Only go as hard/fast as the least experienced fighter can safely go. This may be dictated by the more experienced fighter if he feels that his sparring partner is going harder/faster than he can safely control.

Note: *Your power level is totally separate from your aggressiveness level. You can still be at 100% aggressiveness whilst only using 20% power.*

Protective equipment is highly recommended.

Tapping Out

Tapping out is something you can do when you submit/give up e.g. when a lock starts to hurt. Tap your opponent at least twice so that he feels it. He must disengage immediately. If you cannot reach your opponent, tap the floor. A verbal tap out can also be used, e.g., 'stop'.

Pad/Bag work

With or without a partner, practice techniques on a punching bag or pads (pillows, mattresses etc. can be a low cost substitute). Pad/Bag work allows you to hit something hard.

When sparring, often strikes are 'pulled back' to prevent injury. This trains us not to hit hard. We can hit hard in shadow boxing but we are not actually hitting anything so you do not get the full effect. Pad/Bag work is the answer.

ACHIEVING MAXIMUM POWER

"If you have unshakable balance, correct technique, pinpoint accuracy, lightning speed and incredible force, you will naturally create awesome power."

Bruce Lee

Keep your balance whilst upsetting his. Correct technique will insure this. Strengthen your balance in everyday life by skipping on each foot, standing on one foot while doing things etc.

First learn the technique with proper form in a relaxed manner.

Aim at a recommended target area. Aim 3 inches behind your target.

Increase your speed of movement whilst keeping force. This is improved through repetitive training and muscle conditioning, including stretching. Stay relaxed until the last moment before the impact of the strike.

Target Areas

A good target area is one that will cause sufficient pain and/or disablement when struck, even if the strike is not incredibly forceful. It also needs to be easy to hit, i.e., not a 'pin-point' target.

Point of Chin. A good strike here can knock someone out, and if you miss, then at least you are hitting him in the face.

Eyes. If the eyes are attacked aggressively this can do permanent damage.

Neck/Throat. The neck and/or throat can be attacked with strikes or chokes.

Lower Torso. This includes abdomen, lower ribs and solar plexus.

Groin. Attacking the groin is effective on all genders.

Base of Skull. A good strike here can knock someone out.

Base of Spine. Excessive, but may be necessary in a life threatening situation.

Legs. If you take out his legs, he cannot get up to attack you. When against someone who is not conditioned, anywhere in the leg (including his feet) can cause pain.

Joints. Knees, elbows, shoulders, fingers etc. Apply pressure in the opposite way it was meant to go. Apply slowly for compliance. Apply swiftly and/or increase pressure to break.

YOUR FIGHTING STANCE

At the first sign of confrontation, adopt the fighters' position (FP).

Your Lead Side

If your right leg is forward most, then your right side is your lead and your left side is your rear.

When fighting, have your strong side as your lead most of the time. Most of your strikes come off your lead.

Train on both sides.

Fighters Position (FP)

Initially the FP appears non-aggressive, but it is primed for attack and defense.

Stand with your feet shoulder width apart and take a natural step back. Put a slight bend in your knees. Your body is relaxed with a slight forward lean.

Note: *You step back because it is a non-aggressive gesture. If your intention is to attack as you adopt the FP e.g. an immediate strike, then you would step forward to close distance and attack.*

Find the point at which you are most balanced. To test, have someone push you from the front.

Your hands come up near your head, your lead hand slightly forward more.

Palms open facing in at each other, and about half facing your opponent. Keep your elbows in close to your body.

When engaging keep your teeth together, chin tucked and eyes up.

THE BEST WAY TO WIN A FIGHT... FAST!

Attacking first, fast, hard, and by surprise is the best way to win a street fight. Attack him when he is not ready, and then to keep attacking until you have won. You have won when your opponent is no longer trying to attack you. This could be because he has 'given up' or you have rendered him physically unable to fight. Take advantage of anytime he gets distracted, including whilst either of you are talking.

Beware of Telegraphing

Anything you do that alerts your opponent to your intentions is telegraphing. Show no preparation of movement.

How to Sneak up on Someone

The best way to prevent telegraphing is to attack from behind. Some may think down on this tactic, but you may wish to do this if someone is attacking a friend, if someone is looking to harm you but hasn't found you yet, etc.

Move swiftly and quietly. If possible, crouch down to come in below your target's eye level.

REAR NAKED CHOKE (RNC)

The RNC can cause unconsciousness within 10 seconds. Re-consciousness is as fast.

Encircle your opponent's neck with your right arm. His trachea is at the crook of your elbow. Your right hand grabs your upper left arm, preferably at the biceps.

Put your left hand behind his head and squeeze you elbows together.

If He Tucks His Chin

Force him to expose his neck by pulling up at his eyes or scraping your forearm under his nose.

Applying the RNC on a Tall Opponent

Either jump off the ground to grab his neck or 'cut him down' , e.g., by attacking his groin, then apply the RNC.

If you have at least some hold of him, you can stomp at the back of his knee and/or walk backwards to lower him.

Note: As a general rule is all fighting, never show your back to an opponent.

Applying any choke for longer than necessary may lead to brain damage or even death. Prevent this by releasing as soon as he goes limp (or your training partner taps out). If he is unconscious for more than 20 seconds, seek medical help.

Encourage re-consciousness by lifting his legs so the blood goes back to his head.

STRIKING HIM FROM BEHIND

The best place to strike someone from behind is the base of the skull. This gives the best chance for a knock out. Use a blunt weapon or your palm heel.

Palm Heel

The palm heel is used instead of the fist to prevent personal damage. Some arm reach is lost, but the sacrifice is worth it.

Pull your fingers back out of the way and make contact with the lower part of your palm.

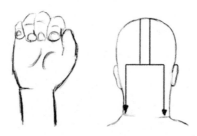

Strike your opponent with as much power as you can to the base of his skull (where the top of his neck meets the bottom of his head). Put your weight behind the strike.

If the strike does not knock him out, rush him or apply the RNC.

RUSHING YOUR OPPONENT

To 'rush' is to quickly close in on your opponent with a flurry of attacks, with the intent of finishing the fight.

Quick Advance

Use the quick advance to quickly close distance and/or increase power in an attack.

With all footwork have both knees slightly bent and relaxed.

Keep your feet close to the ground and move swiftly.

The distance between your feet should be as in the FP whenever possible.

Your front foot steps forward approximately 3 inches.

Immediately slide the rear foot to trail the lead.

When striking with the quick advance your hand moves first and the strike must hit its target before your lead foot lands, otherwise you will lose power.

ELBOWS AND KNEES

Elbows and knees are fast and powerful fight finishers. This is because they are harder and less fragile than the bones in the hand, and they can be delivered with much greater force behind them.

Elbows

Begin in the FP.

Sharply twist your hip and pivot on the ball of your foot (the same side of the elbow you are striking with).

Snap and drive your elbow into his face, preferably his jaw.

Your hand is kept open to expose the bone.

Keep your elbow close to your body and your arm loose until the last moment.

Your wrist stays limp.

As in all strikes, power comes up from the ground and from the pivot in your hips.

For added power, grab your opponent and drive his head into your elbow as your strike.

Knees

Knees can make contact from a variety of angles.

Pull your opponents hair/head/ears down and drive your knee into his face.

Do it more than once consecutively for more damage.

Extend your hips and come up with your toes to increase force. Point your foot and toes down for protection.

A knee to the groin is also very effective. If needed, hold your opponent's shoulders.

ATTACKING COMBINATIONS

A combination is any flowing sequence of attacks. Some examples are:

- Lead palm heel, rear palm heel (1-2)
- 1-2, grab and elbow
- Elbows and knees
- 1-2, choke
- 1-2, elbows and knees, choke
- Elbows and knees, basic trip

1-2 Combination

The 1-2 combination is a lead palm heel, followed by a rear palm heel. In the rush it is used to bridge the gap for the use of elbows/knees/chokes etc.

Note: All strikes can also be used individually i.e. not in combination.

Lead Palm Heel

From the fighter's position, strike straight out.

There is no preparation e.g. do not pull back before you strike.

Your rear hand protects your head.

Strike through him (not push) and then recover by bringing your limb straight back.

Strike with your whole body.

Transfer the force of your legs, waist and shoulder into the strike.

Rear Palm Heel

As you are retracting your lead, thrust your rear palm heel out through your target. Push off your rear foot and torque your hips as you strike. Bend your front leg and bring up your rear leg slightly whilst executing.

Extend your rear shoulder to maximize the reach of your arm for penetrating power.

Related Chapters:

- Elbows and Knees

THE THREE SECOND KO

The person who gets the first good blow in has a much greater chance of winning the fight.

As soon as you sense the fight is inevitable, strike your opponent in the chin, preferably when he is not ready.

Take advantage of anytime he gets distracted, including when either of you are talking.

Often, a good strike to the point of his chin will knock him out, but you should not just strike once in confidence that he will drop. Doing so will leave you vulnerable to counter attacks.

It is better to attack in combination with no initial intent to stop until you are sure you have won.

You have won when your opponent is no longer trying to attack you. This could be because he has 'given up' or you have rendered him physically unable to fight, e.g., he is on the floor.

GUILLOTINE CHOKE

You may come up against a very tough opponent, who will not be put down from your initial attack.

Continuing to aggressively strike for too long will cause fatigue and/or cause damage to you.

If this happens, or before it happens, choke him out.

Either move behind him and use the RNC, or use the Guillotine from the front.

Wrap your arm around the back of your opponents' neck and under the front of it, so that his head is to the side of your torso.

Your palm is facing your own chest.

Ideally, your forearm is under his Adams apple.

Use your other hand to grasp your first hand/wrist/forearm and then pull up into yourself with both hands.

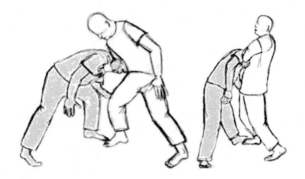

LANDING SAFELY

Another option you have is to force your opponent onto the ground.

But before training in takedowns you must learn how to land safely.

Break Falling

Break Falling is one method of safe landing. It "breaks" your fall by taking the impact on the meaty portions of the body.

Spread the force of the fall, relax your body, and slap the ground.

Keep as much of your spine off the ground as you can and protect your head by tilting it away from the ground.

Side Break Fall

Swing your right arm and right foot across the center line of your body, collapsing your left knee.

When you land, do so on as much of your right side as possible.

Don't let your elbow hit and slap the ground hard.

Your left foot should still be on the ground and your knee should be folded.

As always, practice on the left side also.

Back Break Fall

Squat down to lower yourself closer to the ground.

Arc your back and thrust your groin up toward the ceiling while simultaneously slapping with both hands.

Tuck your chin to your chest to protect your head.

Make contact with the ground on your upper shoulders.

As your confidence increases, don't squat down so much.

Forward Break Fall

Squat down and fall forwards, landing on your forearms with your palms down.

You land in a planking position. Only your forearms and toes should be in contact with the ground.

Increase to falling from a standing position, then jumping etc.

Rolling

In general, rolling is better than the break fall because you will return to your feet.

Sometimes, due to the way you are being forced to the ground, rolling is not possible, e.g., being tackled by the legs, which is why you learn the break fall.

Forward Roll

Put your right foot forward and make your right arm into a sturdy arc.

Swing your right arm hard across your center line.

Tuck your head and roll over your right shoulder.

The pressure should run from your right shoulder, diagonally across your back, ending up somewhere around your left hip.

As you go over bend your left knee so that your momentum brings you back to your feet to face your opponent(s).

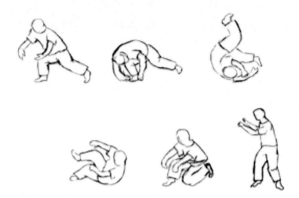

Backward Roll

As you are falling, tuck your chin and collapse your rear leg as if sitting down on your calf. Keep your body curved a loose as you fall backwards and roll over the opposite shoulder of the leg you collapsed. Come out of the roll into the fighter's position to face your opponent(s).

Note: If falling back or to the side you can side break fall and then if able, continue into the backward roll.

Forward Roll with Break Fall

This is useful if there is something preventing you from completing the roll e.g. a wall.

When you go into your roll keep the side opposite your rolling arm perfectly rigid.

Roll across your arm, shoulder, and lower hip. Slap hard to come to a sudden stop.

PUTTING HIM ON THE GROUND

Now that you know how to land safely, you can learn how to put each other on the ground.

Here are some simple methods to take-down your opponent whilst you stay standing, which is always preferred.

Triangle Theory

Triangle theory is a basic balance concept. To put someone on the ground you must upset his balance. Knowing this will also help you maintain your balance.

When standing, your feet make up 2 points of a triangle.

The third point, which can be on either side, is the direction where you are most off balance.

If you are forced towards this third point you will be unbalanced.

If you cannot reposition yourself to regain your balance, you will fall.

Basic Trip

Grab your opponent close, e.g., bear hug, shirt front, or by the shoulders.

Place your foot at his third point behind him, as close to his body as possible without losing your own balance.

Throw/shove him over your leg.

Twist His Head

Where his head goes, his body will follow.

Grab his head by the top and under his chin and twist it towards the floor.

You can combine this with the basic trip.

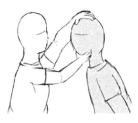

Once He Is On the Ground

Once your opponent is on the ground, stomp him and/or escape.

When attacking someone on the ground, come in from the side.

Stomp his knees, ribs and chest with the heel of your foot.

Stomping the head is excessive but may be necessary in a life threatening situation.

IF HE STRIKES FIRST

If your opponent makes the initial strike, there are a number of techniques/strategies you can use. The one you use will depend on the type of incoming attack and how quickly you are able to react.

Bursting

Bursting is best used against curved attacks e.g. hooks.

Using the power from your legs, explosively move forward (not jumping) whilst blocking and striking at the same time.

The block and strike land simultaneously.

Aim the strike (palm heel) at the chin or upper torso.

Slip, Parry, and Strike

This is one move with 3 components best used against straight attacks e.g. jab, cross, straight punch etc.

As the attack comes in, move your head to the outside of his striking arm and a little forward so you can close in to attack.

Only move it just enough to not get hit. This is the slip.

At the same time, use your hand to brush the strike off. This is the parry and in this instance, is used a secondary defense.

Only move your arm just enough to redirect his strike away from you. It does not go past your shoulder.

If your slip is good, then you may not even make contact with the parry. Also, at the same time, with the hand that isn't parrying, palm heel him. Use the rush i.e. close in with a quick advance and then attack.

Cover and Rush

This is also for side attacks. Cover up and move in to elbow and knee range to neutralize the impact of his strike(s). Then you will attack.

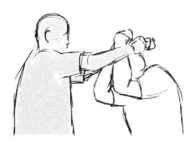

From the fighter's position, lift your elbows up and forward so that your palms are resting/pressing on your ears or forehead.

Your elbows are sticking out in front of you.

If you can, hold your forearms towards the direction of attack.

Keep your eyes up, your chin tucked and your teeth together.

Use the quick advance to close in and rush.

Sprawling

This is a classic Mixed Martial Arts (MMA) technique used to defend against someone tackling you.

As he lunges towards you, kick your legs back and drop your weight onto his upper back.

Arch your back as much as possible and stay on your feet/toes.

Apply the guillotine.

FIGHTING ON

In some circumstances, a fight may go on for an extended amount of time, i.e., over a minute.

Some reasons for this may be:

- The fighters are evenly matched.
- The people fighting do not actually want to fight, e.g., in the school yard.
- Neither fighter is aggressive enough to finish the fight quickly.
- You are sparing (a training simulation).

Whatever the reason, continuing to fight intensely will wear you out. You must 'fight on" at a less intense pace until there is another opportunity to rush.

Note: If he attacks first and you miss the rush opportunity, then you start with fighting on.

ALWAYS HAVE YOUR MINDSET ON ATTACK WITH THE INTENTION OF WINNING.

Even when you are defending, you are thinking of your attack.

Defense is an aid to your attack. Always be on the attack. It is very important.

Parry, then attack.

Move swiftly to avoid being struck, but keep pressing forward.

POSITIONING AND FOOTWORK

Positioning

Use footwork and your surrounding environment to your full advantage. Some examples are:

- Force your opponent into awkward places.
- Adopt the higher ground
- Position your opponent so that the sun/light/smoke, etc. is in his eyes.

Switching

Use the switch to change your lead side.

It is handy to cause confusion in your opponent if he has gotten accustomed to your original lead, but is more commonly used when naturally flowing on after striking.

This is easily done by stepping through e.g. when kicking or in combination.

A quick switch can be made by way of a little jump made as low to the ground as possible.

Quick Retreat

The quick retreat is the same as the quick advance but in reverse i.e. your rear foot moves first.

Note: Never take more than three steps back unless you are sure you know what is behind you.

All Other Footwork

To make side, circular and diagonal movements use the same principles as with the quick advance and retreat.

Keep balanced by keeping your feet low to the ground and maintaining the distance between your feet as best you can.

Never cross your feet.

FRONT KICKS

Lift the knee of your leg up as high as you want to aim (no higher than his groin), and angle it toward the target.

Snap your foot into the target using the ball, bottom or heel of your foot.

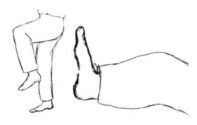

Retract your foot back to the ground along the same path that you extended it.

Shins, knees and the groin are the best targets.

DEFENSE AGAINST STRIKES

Dodging Strikes

If a strike is coming straight at your face and you can't burst or slip, parry and palm heel, then move out of the way. Combine this with parrying if needed. Use footwork and sharp movements from the waist.

Checking

The best defense against kicks is dodging. If dodging is not possible, or you want to close in, use the check. The check works especially well when defending against kicks coming in from the side e.g. Muay Thai.

As the attack comes in lift your leg perpendicular to his. Your shin bone is turned towards his. It will hurt if you are not conditioned.

If you want to close, then lean into the check so you step down towards him and attack.

Note: *The picture shows no intent of closing.*

Defending Against Knees

Block his knee with your arms and if/when possible; drop your elbow into his thigh as he brings his knee up.

If needed, catch and hold onto his leg.

COUNTERS AND FEINTING

Counters

A counter is an attack in reply to an attack. A perfect example of this is the slip, parry, and palm heel.

If you parry and strike (counter) with different hands then it can be done simultaneously, like the burst.

If you parry and strike with the same hand, then strike from where you finish your parry.

Parrying and countering can also be done without your opponent throwing an initial attack. As you advance, parry his lead hand down and immediately follow up with a strike. This works especially well if he holds his guard out too far.

Feinting

Pretend to attack your opponent so that he reacts. By doing so, you can anticipate his response and counter.

The feint must be a real (although partial) attack so he is convinced to react.

Note: Every movement you make should have a purpose. You should always strike for hits, whether they are direct hits, or hits in a sense that you are deducing information. Don't waste energy on misses.

IF YOU BECOME OVERWHELMED

You may become overwhelmed by your opponent. If so, go into the covering up position as described in cover and rush.

As soon as the opportunity arises, attack.

If there is no break, hug him tight, preferably around his arms, and then employ one or more of the following attacks and/or the basic trip.

Head But

Tilt your head slightly downward, clench your teeth, stiffen your neck muscles, and frown. Take aim and lunge forward using your whole body (if possible).

Connect at your target with your forehead. His nose is a good target. Aim to strike using the area one-inch or 25mm above your eyebrow.

To increase force, bend at the middle of your back and lean back a bit before striking.

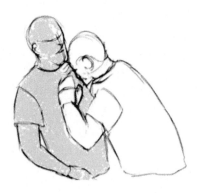

Attack the Eyes

Your opponent's ability to fight will be drastically reduced if he cannot see.

Obscure his vision.

Put your thumb in his eyes, throw things in his eyes, put the sun in his eyes etc.

Attack the Groin

Strike his groin, e.g., with a knee.

Even better is to grab his groin and twist.

This grab and twist method is much more painful than just hitting his groin.

ESCAPING SOMEONE'S GRIP

Use the following techniques when grabbed by surprise. Adjust your reaction to the severity of the situation.

Twist and/or Jerk

Where his thumb meets his fingers is the weakest point. Manipulate your escape through that point. For example, if he grabs your right wrist, then in one swift movement bring your right hand up in a clockwise direction so your palm is facing your face.

In the same movement, turn your thumb towards your face and thrust your hand down to the right to break his grip.

Hit His Forearm Mound

The forearm mound is a cluster of nerves. Find the point halfway between your elbow and your wrist. Halfway between this point and your elbow is the forearm mound. You can see the muscle pop out when you clench your fist.

Hitting this point hard 3-5 times will make most people loosen their grip.

Bend His Fingers

If you get hold of one of his fingers you can easily gain compliance and loosen his grip. Bending and twisting them back towards his wrist is most effective. The little finger is easiest to manipulate.

Finger Split

Grab two of his fingers in one hand, and the other two of his fingers (from the same hand) in your other hand. Separate them.

Attack the Back of His Hands

Use a pen or a similar object e.g. a lighter, and strike the back of his hand, or place it there and rub vigorously.

The lighter could also be used by burning his hand.

Scratch His Cuticle

Scratch him at the point where the bottom of his finger nail meets his finger.

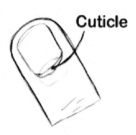

Bite Him

Beware of disease.

Shaking your head while you bite will cause more pain.

Escaping the Bear Hug

The bear hug is when someone wraps his arms tightly around you with the intent of restricting your movements.

Your basic defense is to loosen his grip enough to face him, attack aggressively, and then escape when you can.

ATTACKING TO YOUR REAR

Back Elbow

The back elbow can come straight back from your waist into his lower torso or in a rear hooking motion at his head.

Back Heel

Use on his shin if grabbed from behind or in his ribs or face if you're both on the ground. Drive your heel into your target area.

Side Kick

The side kick can be aimed in any direction and if you add the skip it can be very powerful and useful to cover distance.

If your opponent is close, raise your leg and snap your heel into the target e.g. knee, shin etc. Retract it quickly.

If using the skip, spring forward with your rear leg, allowing your rear foot to replace your lead foot as it springs up into kicking position and simultaneously travels toward your target.

As your back foot replaces your front, straighten your lead leg and kick into your target.

Rear/Side Head But

Slam the back of your head into your target.

ESCAPING CHOKES

Protecting your airway is paramount.

Grab his arm with both your hands and jerk down as hard as you can so you can tuck your chin down and towards his elbow.

From here, work to loosen his grip and attack any way you can e.g. bite, bend fingers, kicks, attack groin etc.

Remember, if he is attacking you from behind then you need to face and attack.

Tucking your chin is good choke preventative.

FIGHTING MULTIPLE OPPONENTS

The first number is your 'team' i.e. two vs. one means two of you against one of him. Communication between team mates is needed to adapt to the situation e.g. if one of you is in trouble, to effectively finish etc.

Two VS One

Advance together on either side of the enemy. As you close in, whoever he isn't focused on goes for his legs whilst the other concentrates on his upper body.

Three VS Two

Advance and close so that the outside two of you are outside of the enemy. Whoever is facing his opponent alone can fight or stall until the other two have finished and can come to his aid.

Even Numbers

One fighter stays in reserve until the enemy has committed their entire force. The reserved fighter then attacks from behind.

One Vs Two or More

Stay on your feet and use your surroundings to create a situation where you are only facing one opponent at a time, including putting them in each other's way.

If you end on the ground (avoid at all costs) move into a corner or against a wall. Use a modified guard in which your legs are not exposed.

Two VS Three

Both of you attack one opponent at a time until you have defeated all three. If you are separated, then fighter 1 defends against two, while fighter 2 fights one on one. Fighter 2 comes to fighter 1's aid when he has finished with his opponent.

STAND UP FIGHTING STRATEGIC GUIDE

Get a weapon

If you can, attack him from behind, either:

- Rear Naked Choke
- Strike the base of his skull

If you have him face on, strike first and knock him out.

If your initial strikes don't KO him, either:

- Choke him out using the RNC or guillotine
- Put him on the ground

If he strikes first, either:

- Burst
- Slip, parry and strike
- Cover and rush
- Sprawl and guillotine

If your initial rush doesn't stop him, fight on until there is an opportunity to rush.

If you become overwhelmed:

- Cover up and attack when possible
- Bear hug him
- Head but, eyes, groin

If grabbed by surprise, either:

- Twist and/or jerk
- Hit his forearm mound
- Attack his hands/fingers

If you are attacked from the rear or side:

- Escape his grip
- Face and attack him

To escape a choke hold:

- Protect your airway
- Tuck your chin towards his elbow
- Attack him
- Loosen his grip
- Escape

If thrown to the ground, either:

- Roll or break fall, then get up
- Cover Up then bring him down

MULTIPLE OPPONENTS STRATEGIC GUIDE

Two Vs One

- Advance at the same time from the sides
- One attacks top whilst other attacks bottom

Three vs. Two

- Advance so two of you are outside the enemy

- One must fight alone until others can help

Even Numbers

- One fighter in reserve until enemy commits entire force
- Reserve fighter attacks from behind

One vs. Two or More

- Escape if possible
- Get a weapon
- Line them up
- Stay off the ground

Two vs. Three

- Both attack one opponent at a time

Related Chapters:

- If He Strikes First
- If You Become Overwhelmed
- Stand Up Fighting Strategic Guide

THANKS FOR READING

Dear reader,

Thank you for reading *How to Win a Street Fight*.

If you enjoyed this book, please leave a review where you bought it. It helps more than most people think.

Don't forget your FREE book chapters!

You will also be among the first to know of FREE review copies, discount offers, bonus content, and more.

Go to:

https://offers.SFNonfictionBooks.com/Free-Chapters

Thanks again for your support.

REFERENCES

AppOpus. (2012). *U.S. Army Field Manual FM 3-25.150 (21-150) COMBATIVES: Expanded Edition*. AppOpus.

DeMile, J. (1977). *Tao of Wing Chun Do, Vol. 2: Bruce Lee's Chi Sao*. Tao of Wing Chun Do.

Filotto, G. (2011). *Systema : The Russian Martial System*. Create-Space Independent Publishing Platform.

Gutierrez, V. (2009). *WingTsun. Chi Sao II*. Sportimex.

Indio, D. (2012). *Mixed Martial Arts Fighting Techniques: Apply Modern Training Methods Used by MMA Pros!*. Tuttle Publishing.

Lee, B. (2008). *Bruce Lee's Fighting Method*. Black Belt Communications.

Lee, B. (2011). *Tao of Jeet Kune Do: Expanded Edition*. Black Belt Communications.

Lung, Haha. Prowant, C. (2000). *Ninja Shadowhand - The Art Of Invisibility*. Citadel Press.

Mamiko, V. (2012). *Systema No Contact Combat*. Varangian Press.

Plyler, D. Seibert, C. (2009) *The Ultimate Mixed Martial Arts Training Guide: Techniques for Fitness, Self Defense, and Competition*. Krause Publications.

Yeo, S. (2011). *Ninjutsu: The Secret Art of the Ninja*. Crowood.

Yimm Lee, J. (1972). *Wing Chun Kung-Fu*. Ohara Publications.

AUTHOR RECOMMENDATIONS

Teach Yourself Self-Defense!

This is the only self-defense training manual you need, because these are the best street fighting moves around!

Get it now.

www.SFNonfictionBooks.com/Self-Defense-Handbook

Teach Yourself Evasive Wilderness Survival!

Discover all the evasive survival skills you need, because if you can survive under these circumstances, you can survive anything!

Get it now.

www.SFNonfictionBooks.com/Evasive-Wilderness-Survival-Techniques

ABOUT SAM FURY

Sam Fury has had a passion for survival, evasion, resistance, and escape (SERE) training since he was a young boy growing up in Australia.

This led him to years of training and career experience in related subjects, including martial arts, military training, survival skills, outdoor sports, and sustainable living.

These days, Sam spends his time refining existing skills, gaining new skills, and sharing what he learns via the Survival Fitness Plan website.

www.SurvivalFitnessPlan.com

amazon.com/author/samfury

goodreads.com/SamFury

facebook.com/AuthorSamFury

instagram.com/AuthorSamFury

youtube.com/SurvivalFitnessPlan

Printed in Great Britain
by Amazon

86110123R00041